CODE

BITE Strike

Jan Burchett and Sara Vogler ● **Jon Stuart**

D1465107

Contents

OXFORD

UNIVERSITY PRESS

Welcome to Micro World

Macro Marvel
(billionaire inventor)

Macro Marvel invented Micro World –
a micro-sized theme park where you have
to shrink to get in.

A computer called **CODE** controls
Micro World and all the robots inside –
MITEs and BITEs.

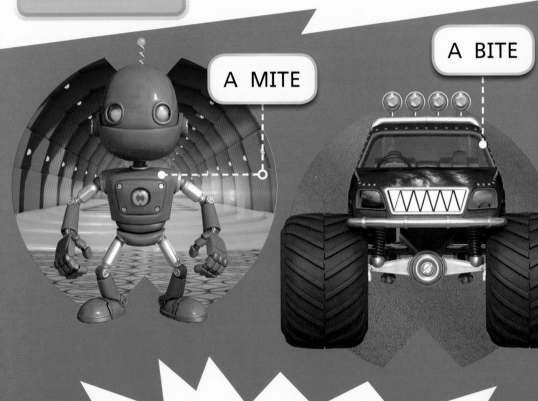

A MITE

A BITE

Disaster strikes!

CODE goes wrong on opening day.
CODE wants to shrink the world.

Macro Marvel is trapped inside the park ...

Enter Team X!

Four micro agents – *Max, Cat, Ant* and *Tiger* – are sent to rescue Macro Marvel and defeat CODE.

Mini Marvel joins Team X.

Mini Marvel
(Macro's daughter)

Together they have to:

- Defeat the BITEs
- Collect the CODE keys
- Rescue Macro Marvel
- Stop CODE
- Save the world!

**CODE key
(3 collected)**

Look at the map on page 4. You are in the Wild Rides zone.

Before you read

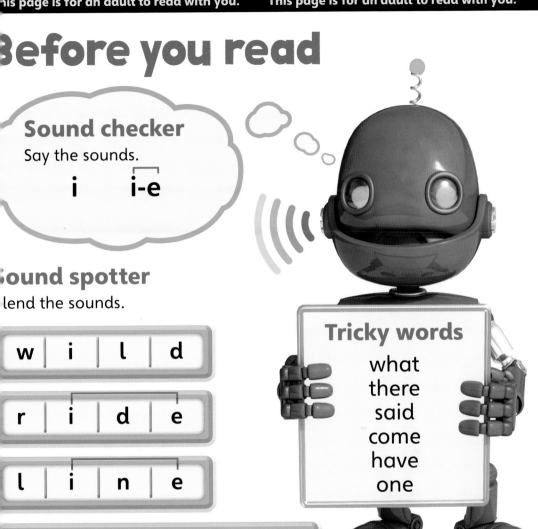

Sound checker

Say the sounds.

i   i-e

Sound spotter

Blend the sounds.

| w | i | l | d |

| r | i | d | e |

| l | i | n | e |

| b | e | h | i | n | d |

Tricky words

what
there
said
come
have
one

Into the zone

What do you think the Wild
Rides zone might be like?

5

Wild Rides

"Let's see what rides there are in the Wild Rides zone," said Mini.

Jump inside one of the fantastic rides.

Take a car, a plane or a train.

Zoom high in the air in the plane.

Take the train and ride the Wild Express.

Get behind the wheel of an amazing car.

The MITEs are there to help you.

Have a good time!

Loop the loop high in the air. Cross the winning line and get a prize.

Now you have read ...
Wild Rides

Text checker

What can you ride in this zone?
Which ride would you choose?
Which do you think is fastest?

MITE fun

Look at page 10. Which ride do you think
will cross the finishing line first? Which do
you think will come second?

Before you read

Sound checker
Say the sounds.

i   i-e

Sound spotter
Blend the sounds.

d	i	v	ed

t	i	m	e

sh	i	n	y

l	igh	t	s

Tricky words

so
like
said
there
what

Into the zone
This story is called 'The Crash'.
Who do you think will crash?

The Crash

Max, Ant and Rex jumped inside the Wild Express train.

Tiger dived into a shiny car
and set off at high speed.

Cat and Mini had a surprise!
Their car turned into a plane!

"We're so high. I like this ride!" said Mini.

"I can see Tiger's car down there," said Cat. "Wait – what's that?"
A monster truck was behind Tiger.

Suddenly, the truck's lights turned red.
"It's the BITE!" yelled Mini.

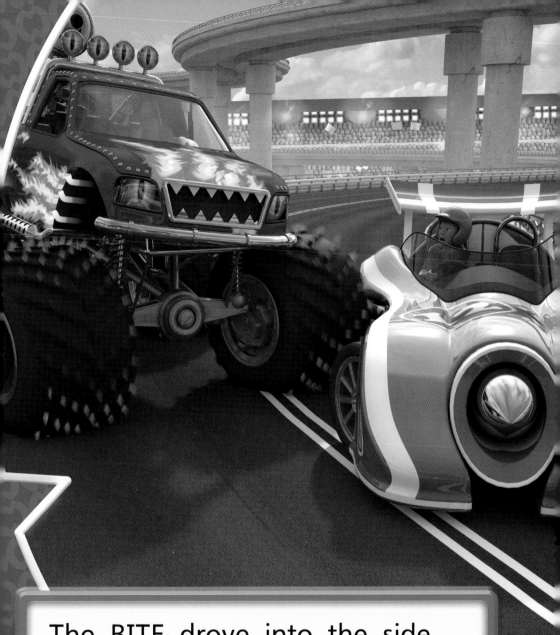

The BITE drove into the side
of Tiger's car.
It was trying to cut his wheels!

"We must help Tiger," said Cat.
The plane dived towards the BITE.
Tiger stopped his car just in time.

The BITE crashed into a tunnel.

Part of the tunnel wall fell down.
The BITE zoomed off.

"That BITE is bad," said Cat.
"Let's chase it," said Mini.
"We need the CODE key."

Now you have read ...
The Crash

Text checker
Mini spotted the BITE, but how did she know what it was?

MITE fun
Why did the BITE crash?

I'll be back!